# Shadows Approach

Derek Vaive

Presentation by *BookLeaf Publishing*

Web: www.bookleafpub.com

E-mail: info@bookleafpub.com

ISBN: 9789358311372

First edition 2023

*To my wife Sam*

*Thank you for always being a willow in the wind*

# ACKNOWLEDGEMENT

The 7 directions, Sam Vaive, Robin Vaive, Kori Vaive, Eli Hyman, Emma Camarda, Michael Pleyte, Ashley Starr, Keith V. Smith, Jack Burton, Egg Shen, Pan, Steve Gray, Tim Ryal, Jay Goldsmith, Corey Staley, Tommy "Flash" Lindquist, and all the brothers and sisters at Pokagon.

# PREFACE

"I desire the things which will destroy me in the end"

~Sylvia Plath

# Metamorphosis

What a familiar story,
it comes with a price,
like all those looming dead
that follow me from town to town,
screams pointing the way
as if time ran backwards
or a history could teach me the endings.
But it's all gone away now,
endlessly lurking in the soils
as I dig further and further,
farthest from a place once home,
this yearning to perform for you,
to act out my fragile calling
like hearts that collide under pressure,
turning every chapter of this
into something I am no longer writing,
another trail weaving through the forest.
I always wanted too many ways to get lost,
but the hourglass is looking lighter these days
and I've got no way out from the dark,
like old ages that draft a story buried,
noted but never hitting quite as hard,
so I'll wait for the late upon receipt,
yet it's still so fresh at the moment,
and I'm far too ripe to pay these dues.

# Holy Men Divide

I flail my arms with violence
going down Route 66,
rusted out Chevy Sport,
Limping,
just passed that town near
the dingy pizza parlor,
a boarded schoolhouse,
a hollowed out strip mall,
Defiled,
but only on nights
when the shots destroyed worlds.
Until I asked for it to stop.
That day we realized skin dies,
Relentless,
aching for drink to devour
enemy territory as protest,
that was long after we crossed
borders full on stolen prayers,
Reckoning,
behind us every town burning,
like children who embrace
out of mere gesture.
I left for good that night.
Converted,
one more buzzing insect

leaning from a barroom balcony,
fixed on that wounded road
with a million translucent eyes,
Retching,
a supper that goes terminal,
like being martyred
by a martyr.

# Resisting in Swan Song

It's underneath now,
striding up the mountain,
one by thousands,
round after round,
brewing a disgust,
taunting a surrender,
breeding something cold
something unhinged
something calculated,
it is the innocence draining,
a pride slowly decaying,
like weeks spent wide-eyed
the better future never waning,
it is Redcaps perched up and waiting,
like the Goldfinch,
that familiar warble forever feigning.
And when it pulls and stumbles aside,
standing one drawn out weighted line
over and over and over,
its gravity brisk
and full of unearthed bodies,
brimming with spirit,
until it catches a glimpse,
catches that sobering false-heartedness,
smoke after smoke

it breathes far too deep,
seeing itself perish in crippled mirrors.
Only if it could look passed the violence,
the adulteration,
its dawning consternation,
with still looming over-worlds
always dark and underrated,
like a flame in the wildwood
or another episode of grief,
one more Goldfinch
taking flight without wind,
clutching the brink so deep
no melody could ever break loose,
this will be Aida's portrait of a pastime,
or just a delicate thought,
like thirteen bullets calling for contact,
if not for lament
and the desire of the dead.

# Ode to the Cannibals

I never heard a thing like that before,
never knew something like this could happen,
never thought the boldness would birth itself,
raw umbilical cords ready to sever,
all things I get on my knees for,
everything hoped for
dreamed for and prayed for.

Gone now,
like that winter that never ends,
I forgot it was possible,
my oversight never thinking it probable,
always confident it was not comprable,
nevertheless all of it has changed,
linked like letters in constant range
of one another
but always inevitably estranged,
everything fought for,
worked for and yearned for,
transformed like a summer breeze
that always bends unremarkably heated,
I was taught it was feasible,
learned about what made me agreeable,
looking always to a future of the foreseeable,
but now I'm not so sure.

I never heard it quite like this before,
never knew it could exist,
never thought the warmth could mourn itself
if only to resist,
all those things that drive it fast,
farther from one another,
further from that last hope
that last dream
that last plea and fading gleam,
the last thing I might ever do,
a final token with breath left behind,
warnings to teach and maybe rewind,
as beasts devour hearts anyway,
gluttonous because they prefer it
with sharpened teeth to grind,
for the record I wish it to be certain,
nurture stays kin in ways that will bind,
but my truth is my truth,
nothing else seems pertinent,
our nature made now
must be born with unkind.

# Tetrapod

The village sea,
it traps this heart
in the most stale of places,
confusing the confessions
to where I want to be,
aging oceans making lizards
buy oxygen, breathing
between the moons
that make gurus naïve,
this is adoption,
life wet with sorrows,
when a touch can tremble
and one kiss begs for another,
but I forgot how to levitate,
and I don't pretend how to climb—
in this rooted house,
it falls faster
with all the new dawns,
crumbling my lust full
from language sickness,
poised now
to purchase a summers fade,
mounds of cash, stripped
underneath the turbid grove
that turn elders brittle,

this is abandonment,
death soaked in pining,
but this time I'll never spend it all,
or leave home
before it becomes dusk again.

# Accompanist and the Underground

Dingy, dark and nicotine fogged,
basements like sunken tombs,
the clutter of littered rugs
enriched from mythical stains,
always delinquent,
like the city landfills
they were rescued from.
These free spaces eat tourists—
gestation of the craftsman—
hours of reckless floating
in crystalline daze,
fluent in seasoned glass,
kindly bringing false order
or drowning in self distortion;
some kind of drive
through channels electric,
but only in wounded chariots,
memories hazy,
like those cryptic boroughs
of dark and consummate dingy.
Monuments brim on early dying
and ballads of remembrance,
the alleys flow with legacy
for all and also none,

as the accompanist must be,
bound for keeps
to perform with shadow,
at home with the chorus
but never quite fully done.

# False Dichotomies

Running comes heavy
without smoke to breathe,
the satisfaction of frailty,
a virtue that arrives tactful
and with sunken cheeks.

I thought I could feel.
I thought I could taste.
I never thought days
would grow ancient,
mellowed with seasons
moldy and middling.

Peddling with ease
means losing little hands,
like all those boy kings
that giggle on their bikes,
stark they ride straight
but never pass in pairs.

I thought I would eat.
I thought I would see.
I never knew the nights
had so many barren suns,
shining for a bold end

but built to ever-last.

Drinkers,
the beggar,
a pimp,
varicose veins filled
with too much dead science,
playing out their cons,
pockets brimming
with a lingering violence.

One more drag,
one final hit,
times that collect
minutes hidden away,
those dim corners
married to fetish,
and thrills served up
On food stamps.

I thought I could speak.
I thought I would hear.
I never realized.
It was one or the other.

# The Psychology of Peter Pan

She never answered my question
that night on the rusted balcony,
instead she sat on it for days
and fed it tablets of sleepy white chalk,
while my stomach begged me
to open the fridge and claim something,
holy like the great ascetics of passed,
Siddhartha or Ghandi,
I just waited for the pangs to hit
like the Ford Sedan that silenced Dean.
No words echoed around my skull,
bouncing off the remnants
of angst-ridden adolescence,
as if Kurt Cobain took to the stage
one last time to shriek,
"Here I am, entertain me."
All I can do is stick around
with these nature boy legs,
until the great preserver is dissected
out of boredom or discontent,
we scraped our bony knees
on the art deco tile floor,
as tongues dropped like Dick Clark's
contorted ball of light,
counting down to fresh starts.

And the whole time answers sat
silent in the cool solitude
of all those fears we kept
hidden in the humming icebox,
but I don't want my Wendy
to grab a beer
and grow up without me.

# Personal Temples Exposed

Time after time again,
The kills come bittersweet,
Jaded but with remorse,
There is nothing to show,
Nothing ever amounts
With raw innocence spilled,
It becomes a new disease,
But I'm on the hunt now,
Even though I finally see
The bars of my own cage.

# Butchers Never Go Hungry

Cover all shrinking tables,
wolves wait on the other side,
they want to lunge broad,
strike for their kill,
with eyes full on death,
stomachs loathing escape,
sober spirits that turn
connection to nightmare,
cutting skin from bone.
Watch the expanded rooms,
in every wolves den
bodies lifeless lay
to wither disclosed,
tempered by the blades
in their lasting mouths,
gods spouting wounds
that refuse to heal,
while faithless they lurk
over and above again.
Strike at injured windows,
where wild brutes serve
boundaries to abide,
guarding non-entity
as departed watchers
finally honor the lamb,

the grey shapes counting
minutes till' slumber,
their lawful perfection
a gift to the world,
as nothingness burns
toward the floor,
because the moon
is the only pure thing
they have left.

# Scoring New Skin

Remember that day like yesterday,
it was frigid and ire,
officers screamed on rented time,
peeled back scabs to reveal
all the unknown worlds I wear,
but maybe I should just keep them
in a jar next to the prison bed,
those silhouettes making future me
out of sores that take on thunder,
a troublesome process that looks
to the streets for another drug,
where gazing is always tradition
from those nearly ended,
and my organs daily fight
for another uncertain remedy,
but the dust never settles
and I best be getting back soon.

# Reunion

There he was again,
hidden always
until I needed him,
approach from behind
his only custom,
turning
I saw those eyes,
so black they could light
up a starless night,
his skin shedding off,
melting from the bones,
he reached out
like I was his barge,
"It's my birthday!"
He kept at it,
"Got something for me?"
I performed a body search,
frantic—
like our America—
but my pockets sprang
to instruct my heart
for a breakdown,
"You got anymore?"
A pause,
lifetimes passed,

"That's all I got,"
a smirk,
twist of the head,
an irritation,
"You want some rock?"
The seconds ran fierce,
this became a haunt,
another lifetime
that ran me down,
his next stalk
to be bewildered,
leaving me without
my vertebra,
swift and efficient
as was his only custom,
and that's how he liked it,
it was me the whole time,
but I can only wonder,
as we disappear
together down his drag,
like it had never been.

# In-Laws

They all sit around the table with criticism in
their eyes,
dressed to the nines to worship their kind,
like Evangelicals knocking at 9am on a Sunday,
ready to force feed me passages that can tell the
future,
those holy tongues that only read from fresh
paper.

They only really banter about how they wish
they could be,
waiting for me to make a mistake while they
reach over
and around for the next plate of modernity,
like I was the safety zone in a game of
neighborhood tag,
the talk running so fast now I can't keep up,
like that one time I partied with porno personnel
and collapsed from the cheapness of it all.

"So you play a little music, huh?"
I wonder if they really want to see my insides
fill up this dinner table with battery acid,
as I scream out all my lungs across the room,

a subtle way to let them know I don't just play a
"little,"
not in the sense that anything "little" in my
world
might consist of toning it down to ten beers and
a couple Adderall.

I'm not just a hobbyist that plays a little bit here
and there,
not in the sense of an average person singing
along to top 40…
Gospel…
Or the castration of modern country music—
during a drive to the overpriced salon—
might be…
No…
No, any attempt to justify or explain the nature
of expression,
or a cathartic experience like it was the best drug
on Earth—
even better than a five second or ten or even 20
second orgasm—
would be just a failed and faulty attempt to join
the congregation.

So they all sit around me waiting for the mistake
to greet them,
as if I didn't watch the Jersey Shore or cheer for
the Yankees,

God help me if they finally figure out I was a progressive,
truthfully they don't want to talk about anything like that,
all I can do is choke my knife and fork with a billboard smile,
nervously stuttering like it was post-prom in the bedroom,
"An-an-and I'm also vegetarian."
…And that's everything that they needed.

# The Pantomime

Without a sound I told myself
that I want the pain to end,
I even wore it on my wrist
like His Favourite Pastime,
now a silver plated medical bracclct.
I was Caught In The Rain
on A Busy Day,
Busted Johnny Troubles Doing His Best,
silent but Making a Living.
Between Showers I began to write
but forgot all the periods,
wishing for the moment when I
could read it on my eyes and
be The Face On The BarRoom Floor.
I think I'll spell out the future
with Laughing Gas and tears,
as the pens run dry,
empty wells driving a toxic family
toward squalor of City Lights,
built on the sound of screaming
stomachs and Those Love Pangs.
I said I want to see it rush
out of me like an underage drinker
Caught In a Cabaret,
the party to end all parties,

everyone shoving for the door,
like Kid Auto Races At Venice,
and spilling their courage
on the floor along the way.
I want to see it dance
on the walls,
the Tango Tangles,
like a bull failing to spike
the red curtain that dangles,
tempting my two-step to stutter
like a divorcée square dancing
at local saloons during midlife crisis.
I dare myself to try that dance
with these new shoes,
The Masquerader
and His New Profession,
a Gentlemen Of Nerve,
every step for me to trip
like a 1970's freak-out,
while the Grateful Dead play
"Touch of Grey" in the background,
the room spinning and spinning.
But that isn't as much fun
as the tilt-a-whirl at the county fair,
Recreation only coming around
to bleed me of money,
while the sweat soaked,
beer gutted carnie,
with mosquito bite scabs

nabs my wad of cash
and delivers his greasy grin,
a typical Mabel At The Wheel.
Another dare to peel out my eyes,
use them to watch the pain
splatter these walls I just covered
with coats of fresh paint,
brushed on to seal up
all the Twenty Minutes Of Love,
woes in poorly scribbled scratchings
I wrote to other lovers
on bar napkins and bounced checks,
insufficient funds that paid
for every vision of loss
conceived as The Fatal Mallet.
I kept saying I want the pain to end,
wired under burning hands,
but I could only keep it up until
I forced a Knockout, aka TKO.
I dared myself twice over
only because I'm here to say
it can only get worse,
Cruel Cruel Love,
the one true Thief Catcher,
it sews mouths shut
like a Night in the Show,
makes me feel like The Pilgrim,
but this is His Prehistoric Past,
I can only hope this silver bracelet

can yell loud enough to catch me,
cause' I put my last buck
in the balmy tip jar
that protects His Trysting Place,
and realized that I became
the best Charlie Chaplin
had ever taught.

# Personal Temples Exposed
## Again

On this autumn day
More killers like me
Swim to the shores,
Bands of beaches where sanity
Plays and hope like a question
Becomes colorless and idle,
I know the story of boredom,
And a fate resigned
To lovers in starstruck worlds,
The ruin of cheap thrills
Is a train with no rails,
But the jury awaits
And even though I'm alone
My mind unwinds and you
Must know why.

# Bipolar II

When the reflecting abyss
like a timepiece waits close,
that's when hailstorms come
and hollow out this shelter,
like one final exhale
of a fresh corpse,
where devils wait in ache
to play the sorted line,
that reflecting abyss
like a sink without pipes,
it feeds these roaring tides,
nibbles up the shedding worship,
greets it all with undoing,
the echo of this abyss,
its needless spirits
tearing the days apart,
when wildfires go brightless
and all the shaded places
begin to cast shadows,
that's when sheets call
but the dreams never answer.

# When the Last Grave is Dug

I wonder how you found your way?
The steps taken when and why?
We could talk it over coffee,
do you take sugar and cream?
I prefer it like the shirts I wore,
a sensibility tight and tough at the seams.

I guess a cup of tea will have to do.
Some honey perhaps, cardamom,
maybe a slice of cake too?
Oh, how it shines with warmest welcome.
I know I'm guilty of thinking it true,
even reaching for an apple at times,
sometimes more than just two.

Ah, the process of pretend.
The sending off of fitted smiles,
manners reserved nightly
by poverty of all the worthwhiles.
Leave it to me to ask the questions,
since I ask all the worst ones.
The printed effigies of stories old,
remarks that weathered hot summers
until these eyebrows grew cold.
I think you wish for more dates to swim,

but never mind all that now,
It's time to sink six foot and three,
please never forget me at the stone
as you drink your coffee or tea.

# Truth is Cheap

The truth always seemed to be
a cheap motel paid by the hour,
man with no teeth standing
behind a bullet-proof window,
fantasizing about all the things
he wished he could watch you do,
while he licked his fingers,
counting the twenty bucks
you just put in his pocket,
like a bad 80's flick.

The truth always seemed to be
a cheap pair of gold plated earrings
you bought your girlfriend
for her thirty-sixth birthday,
as she smiled and hugged you
because you remembered,
but didn't give you a kiss
because she knew they were fake.

The truth always seemed to be
a cheap leather bomber jacket,
cracked instead of faded,
but you wore it to the party anyway,
since all those biker types

seem to get a lot of women,
while you sat home cocktailing
with Hemingway or Vonnegut,
but they don't really warm
your bed quite as well.

> Not quite as well as the feel of skin on
> skin
> or as real as a pus ridden scab.
> Not quite like the time you were
> punished on a Saturday
> for peeing in a cup.
> Or when you wore shades for a week
> because you happened
> to look in the wrong direction at the
> right time.

Truth is cheap because last night
your wife told you the reason
there are still no children
is she was forced in college,
but you wish she hadn't told you now,
it's far too heavy to want to try.

# Gilded Age Revisited

This chamber walks with meter,
sterilizing the below forms,
aching for a stainless cosmos.

Masses need bigger…

Unbound coalitions peddle
like hawks that claw at our eyes,
once exposed leviathans
doting and bolster ancient kinds.

Masses need better…

All the tenors that stuff
us little piggy's with humility,
so full we gag violently,
retching the forward steps
to possess all the new media.

Masses need faster…

Blocs that stroll with devotion,
abandoning safety for programming,
their marked desires
chilled with mania reverence,

shaved apes slashing at the doors,
coaxing us to watch more screens.

The masses want bigger…

A club that takes notes
on every hard trigger,
replacing the switches
with powered hot shells,
covert and inadequate,
all the children convert
and foam at the mouth.

The masses want better…

Our next gorge becoming
the pedagogy of superior client,
urns crammed with untitled strays,
enclosed by the deep of industry,
all those waves that secure
entitled creatures from basements,
a rubbish marching our panic
to the next outlet mall.

The masses want faster…

Wars fought for the glory,
always a lack in the core
to return for more ammo,

a dawning of high frequency,
the last fortunes read urgent
from layers of glowing glass,
recouping it only spawned
by the droning hum of fashions
to all those locks without doors.

The masses feel satisfied…

# Taking Out What's Left

When I turned
the process started
with a nod and two
pours of bourbon,
washing down the fear
that grabbed me
by the arms,
like my father did
the moment I called
a perfect stranger
a complete idiot.

I press that day
against the front
of my eyes,
as if I was peaking
into someone else's
world from the blink
of a microscope,
the light sneaking in
but my mind running
out from the backdoor,
brackish from this tavern.

But this was my world

and it felt so far away,
arms going numb,
begging him to let go,
the grip tightening,
shoulders popping,
time running out
of my wire frame
like a marathon
that had no finish line.

Turning I called
for another drink,
the bartender smiled
and I knew I was cut,
I winked a working eye,
ignoring the crafty pint
that sat far too close.

I wanted a night out
but it was adrift
back in that telescope,
lost by a little boy
who couldn't keep
his mouth shut,
I cursed and slugged off,
dragging toward the exit,
hankering at my heels,
making a single bargain.

A single promise,
a single drink,
one double wink,
looking behind
and finally leaving
that little boy's side.

# Personal Temples Exposed
## III

Working the nights,
Day after day,
It's time to talk of
These heavy breathings,
All these nightly dealings,
Of all the persons reeling
For another poison
To swallow their emptiness,
The silent end of all things
Sacred and mediocre.
Far and away this world
Clenched for some depth,
Hazy fantasies built out
On the fear of dust,
Or a faith in trees
With colorless leaves,
Deep as hell
But tall as the sky.
My will blurring the lust,
Prolonged and deranged,
A never ending perversion,
Like streams bloated by ads,
Endless production that grips
Personal temples exposed.

But let's talk of something else,
Things that truly live,
Something that really gives,
Gives it all with no mind,
To what's in store
For the people that want
More and more and more.
Let's talk of the never winters,
Why many of us killers crack,
Become surrendered or splinter,
Let me see the ones
Who bathe in all this hollow,
Never thinking why
Horizons no longer appear,
Unless they bleed out and follow.

Let me see that final one in bed today,
Say goodbye while they sit and pray,
I won't move or voice a thing,
Only dare this silence now grown,
Gazing through holes up above,
That glimmer of places unforeseen,
My torments gifted but never loaned,
Persisting shadows I'll forever own.